Let Me Love You

Let Me Love You

POETIC BIBLE TRUTHS ABOUT GOD

ERIC ZACK

RESOURCE *Publications* • Eugene, Oregon

LET ME LOVE YOU
Poetic Bible Truths About God

Copyright © 2024 Eric Zack. All rights reserved. Except for brief quotations in critical publications or reviews, no part of this book may be reproduced in any manner without prior written permission from the publisher. Write: Permissions, Wipf and Stock Publishers, 199 W. 8th Ave., Suite 3, Eugene, OR 97401.

Resource Publications
An Imprint of Wipf and Stock Publishers
199 W. 8th Ave., Suite 3
Eugene, OR 97401

www.wipfandstock.com

PAPERBACK ISBN: 979-8-3852-3346-5
HARDCOVER ISBN: 979-8-3852-3347-2
EBOOK ISBN: 979-8-3852-3348-9

Where indicated, Scripture quotations are taken from Scripture taken from the New King James Version®. Copyright © 1982 by Thomas Nelson. Used by permission. All rights reserved

Table of Contents

Preface vii
Introduction xi

About God: I Will Deliver 3
The Temple of God 6
But God 8
God's Realm 10
Today Is the Day of Salvation 12
Beside 16
Outside of Time 20
It's His Design 22
Captured in the Stars 24
God Stays the Same 26
This Is How God Works 30
Saving Souls 32
I Loved You First 34
God So Loves You 36

The Bible: The Mysteries of the Bible 40
You Have to Recognize 42
The Light of the Gospel 44
The Bible's Your Basic Guide 46
Feed on Good Food 48

Surrendering: A New Opportunity 52
I Can't 54

Table of Contents

                    Broken 56
                    Broken, but Renewed 58
                    My Life Is Your Life 60
                    Stretch Marks 62
                    Faith Possessor 64
                    The Purpose of Suffering 66
                    Right There Beside 68

<u>The Church</u>:   Passive Christians 72
                    The Seven Churches 75
                    It's Done 78
                    You Can Come Directly to Me 80
                    Time to Ripe 82
                    The Seal of God 84

About the Author 86

Preface

Welcome to my private collection of Christian poetry spanning five total volumes and 173 original, unique poems that I have written over the past thirty years of my life. Each volume deals with key aspects of Christianity and Holy Bible truths that have been revealed to me during my personal struggles. I have organized each one of these into an easy-to-read-and-follow format. Certain lines and stanzas in each of these poems will also have specific Bible verses referenced if you prefer to investigate further, meditate, or dive deeper into the Word.

Volume 1 focuses on God, the Bible, and surrendering. Volume 2 describes Jesus Christ and the need to be born again. Volume 3 highlights important Christian tenants that support living life to its fullest, such as grace, faith, choice, prayer, life, and blessings. Volume 4 depicts evil such as rebellion, pride, Satan, disease, death, and hell. And finally, volume 5 completes my collection with living for the future by applying Christian beliefs and putting this lifestyle into practice in serving others. It covers topics such as the Church, correction, redemption, finding purpose, the rapture, heaven, and the end of times.

I have generally written these poems whenever I had ideas or inspirations come to me and when I had the time to process them, sit down, and compose them (preferably in an uninterrupted manner). Although their actual chronological order has been lost, I feel that there is great benefit in how these poems have been organized for your understanding and reading pleasure. My brain seems to work in this manner by compartmentalizing related topics

PREFACE

together. My intention was to document many of my own personal experiences along with my spiritual growth journey, not that I am anyone special in that respect. I'm just an ordinary person whose life experiences have opened my eyes to Jesus at an early point in my young adult life due to certain circumstances. I am so grateful for what has happened in my life and that I was chosen worthy by Jesus to suffer through extreme emotional pain. This has directly led me towards Him. My mom's death was absolutely the worst thing that has ever happened to me; yet in retrospect, it was absolutely the best thing that has ever happened to me. This stark dichotomy remains quite perplexing to me. But I have always wanted to learn what the truth is.

My typical poetry style is to tell an impactful story with powerful emotional details that describe a specific defined topic; and most of them possess some rhythm and rhyming pattern based on the melodies of contemporary music. My hope is that they inspire and speak to you and specifically the younger generation—who might appreciate this form of expression. Most of my poems have been adapted as such, changing the lyrics of these songs to reveal important Bible truths. These melodies are also referenced next to my poem titles. But all of these poems are stand-alone, in that without the melody, they should still make perfect sense. Most of my poems are nonfictional (based on real-life experiences as either being autobiographical or biographical in context); while some are completely fictional (made-up to highlight a particular truth). None of these types really matter in order to highlight the main theme of each poem, nor have these been revealed. One secret I have learned over the years about growing closer to Christ is found in Rom 10:17: "So then faith *comes* by hearing, and hearing by the word of God" (NKJV, italics original). This can be accomplished in many ways and whichever ways you choose; these are pleasing to Him.

I considered my life pretty normal growing up until my mom's death. Then seemingly overnight, my world fell apart, and I felt lost and confused. I didn't know what was happening to me. I asked typical questions like, Why me? and, Why now?,

PREFACE

but nothing was revealed to me. Shortly thereafter, my stepfather struggled with alcoholism as a way to self-medicate and numb the emotional pain that he was feeling. And the four of us kids were left to fend for ourselves for our own survival.

I returned to college but barely passed the remaining semesters of my first degree. Nothing as serious as this has ever occurred to me before or ever since thankfully. I was surviving one day at a time and learning valuable lessons as I went through the grieving process internally and privately. It was a slow process for me, as I was still learning who I was, developing into who I wanted to become, all while being a young teenager at heart. All of a sudden, I had to grow up and do so really fast . . . and on my own. Poetry was the only thing that worked for me. Back then, no one had cell phones, and the internet was just created a few years prior to this. Moreover, all of my childhood friends were back in my hometown or away at another college. None of my new college acquaintances could understand what I was going through. Indeed, I felt all alone. Poetry was my only outlet. Putting my emotions down on paper seemed to give these abstract things actual weight, relevance, and true acknowledgment. It also allowed me to literally (physically) and figuratively (emotionally) store my emotions away—as if to feel them, deal with them, learn from them, and then move on from them.

My original intention was simply to try to heal myself—deep down knowing that if I continued to bottle up these emotions over time, I would eventually explode just like a boiling pot of water in a kettle on the stovetop. Introverts need time, privacy, and quiet to process difficult experiences. I did not trust anyone enough to share these vulnerabilities with—for fear of judgment, criticism, or simply being dismissed. I never thought my poems would ultimately be worthy of sharing with others to help them in some way. In the midst of tragedy, you can only think of yourself. However, once you pass through that tragedy, you eventually regain a sense of others in the world and can see life and future possibilities and new opportunities more clearly. My hope and prayers are that my poems can help some of you in whatever you are facing today, whether it be serious or trivial, permanent or temporary, or spiritual, psychosocial, and/or physical. I now realize that Jesus was the only one who could heal me and not as a result of my own efforts. My efforts only proved to be futile attempts to try to do what only God can do. I have learned this valuable lesson to let go of certain things that I cannot control.

    I have continued writing poetry on a regular basis about life's many experiences, topics, and questions. It has become and remains to be a strong coping mechanism for me when dealing with "life." I have continued to develop and refine my writing abilities and have strengthened my art by adding, practicing, and improving on many tools in my toolbox, so to speak. Sharing these Christian poems has become my priority given today's troubling times with so many broken and lost people. Jesus is the answer to all of your questions!

Introduction

Welcome to the first volume of my Christian poetry collection. It is entitled *Let Me Love You: Poetic Bible Truths About God*. This collection focuses on the Divine and His ways, specifically about God, the Holy Bible, surrendering, and the Church. Ultimately, it is your choice (and your choice alone) as to whether or not you open the door to God, Jesus Christ, and the Holy Spirit. He will not force His way into your life. He gave you free will, an absolutely amazing gift to be your own boss. It is my understanding that God does not directly bring devastation into your life, that it is in fact the direct result of Satan and his hatred towards you, being made in the image of God Himself. But certainly, there are many circumstances that God allows to enter into your life that may impact you, to test your faith, and to bring you to the end of yourself in order to surrender to Him and His ways. But you have the free will to decline His invitations. Fortunately, I was broken enough to surrender, having no other way out of my tragedy.

The first section in this book begins with God. God is so many things: holy, perfect, love, eternal, the Creator, omniscient, omnipresent, omnipotent, and the ultimate judge or "boss" of all things. His ways are always the best ways and the correct ways. Anything apart from this is rebellion and sin. We are not worthy of God, but He created a pathway for us to be near to Him.

The second section describes the Holy Bible. The Holy Bible is actually the Word of God; it is written by humans throughout early history, but it is indeed God-breathed. Every word in the original Hebrew and Greek languages is accurate and purposeful.

INTRODUCTION

As a Christian, knowing the Holy Bible is very important. This is how we learn about and develop our relationship with Christ—who He is, how He works, what does He expect from us. The Word of God is also our spiritual weapon against evil in this world. God is triune; the Trinity, God the Father, God the Son (Jesus Christ), and God the Holy Spirit, remains a significant mystery that cannot be explained. All that is required is blind faith—that is, belief without evidence.

The third section deals with the act of surrendering to Christ. This is a necessary step for most people to come to and to receive Christ as your Savior. If you can handle something yourself, then why would you ever need a Savior? God is in the business of saving souls. This is what He cares about most. He wants to spend eternity with you. He loves you. He created you. Many of us eventually come to surrender through the difficult and unpleasant process of suffering, regardless of the type of suffering one may experience such as physically, emotionally, spiritually, socially, or whatever.

Finally, the fourth section pertains to the Church. The Church is not necessarily a physical building, but rather a collection of believers in the world who worship and trust God. God cherishes His Church and uses all of us to actualize His will in our lives in order to help others. We are all called to do different things. We all have unique spiritual gifts, talents, skills, personalities, and characteristics. Achieving satisfaction, joy, and success in your life comes when you realize, utilize, and maximize these things to the best of your ability to benefit others.

Thank you and may God bless you. Please enjoy!

ABOUT GOD

I Will Deliver

(Adapted from the melody of "Survivor" by Destiny's Child)

If left to your own devices, then you're a debtor
But with My blood, I purchased you; so, you're no longer
                                                       Eph 2:13
I desire a relationship with you, please consider
I gave up everything for you; I'm your martyr
I even sent My spirit to be with you, your advisor   Acts 9:17
I created an eternal way for you to bring order
I want to give abundant life to you, so fulfilling   John 10:10
If you trust, believe, and accept My Crucifixion

I will deliver if you drink from My cup   Matt 26:28
I will adopt you, I'm your acquitter
I'm your forgiver; submit to My ways
I gave you life and I'll keep on providing   Gen 2:7
I will deliver if you drink from My cup
I will adopt you, I'm your acquitter
I'm your forgiver; submit to My ways
I gave you life and I'll keep on providing   Gen 2:7

See the unseen, I'll allow you; I'm unveiling
All that you need I'll supply to you, My provision   Phil 4:19
Beyond your dreams, I'll surprise you; this is surpassing
I have a special plan for you
   designed since the beginning   Jer 29:11
Still waters and green meadows for you, part of My flock Ps 23:2
I'll return for all to see with My crown, My peace unlocks
The rapture, then watch their response; yes, it'll be clear
You'll rise in the air because I want you so near   1 Thess 4:17

I will deliver if you drink from My cup
I will adopt you, I'm your acquitter
I'm your forgiver; submit to My ways

Let Me Love You

I gave you life and I'll keep on providing
I will deliver if you drink from My cup
I will adopt you, I'm your acquitter
I'm your forgiver; submit to My ways
I gave you life and I'll keep on providing

I'll provide you with rest, that is if you request	Matt 11:28–29
You must confess, profess, and then possess	Jas 5:16
My grace will surpass	2 Cor 9:14
Faith and love will undoubtedly overflow	
My grace will surpass	
The merciful shall receive, actually	Matt 5:7
My grace will surpass	
Jesus' return is soon, we're in between	Matt 24:42
My grace will surpass	
But for non-believers, the end of humanity	2 Cor 6:14
My grace will surpass	
You may see My face and not just My silhouette	
You're My elect, so let go of any regrets	Eph 1:5–8

I will deliver if you drink from My cup
I will adopt you, I'm your acquitter
I'm your forgiver; submit to My ways
I gave you life and I'll keep on providing
I will deliver if you drink from My cup
I will adopt you, I'm your acquitter
I'm your forgiver; submit to My ways
I gave you life and I'll keep on providing

I want you to understand and not abandon My Ten Commandments
Alongside Myself, I designed you to reign with Me fundamentally

I will deliver if you drink from My cup
I will adopt you, I'm your acquitter
I'm your forgiver; submit to My ways
I gave you life and I'll keep on providing

Let Me Love You

I will deliver if you drink from My cup
I will adopt you, I'm your acquitter
I'm your forgiver; submit to My ways
I gave you life and I'll keep on providing

I will deliver if you drink from My cup
I will adopt you, I'm your acquitter
I'm your forgiver; submit to My ways
I gave you life and I'll keep on providing
I will deliver if you drink from My cup
I will adopt you, I'm your acquitter
I'm your forgiver; submit to My ways
I gave you life and I'll keep on providing

Let Me Love You

The Temple of God

(Adapted from the melody of "Hymn for the Weekend" by Coldplay)

Were you aware that God picked you?	Rom 8:33
Your body's His temple, a river runs through	1 Cor 6:19–20
Designed purpose together anew	
So, He can live within	1 Cor 3:16

Just like if guests were coming, head's up
You'd hurry to clean the place right up
Your body's a gift, protect it much
You must be so careful

So, drink less alcohol, exercise some more
Stay away from cigarettes and all that's related to this

Stress will weigh you down	
So tired and weak, run down	
This creates sicknesses	Ps 107:20
Certainly not God's wish for you	

The devil tries to amplify your sins to terrify, terrify, terrify
Instead cherish God, glorify, and qualify, qualify, qualify

So, drink more water, get out in the sun	
And sleep much more, disease undone	
And then surround yourself with fun	
To reverse this aging curse	Eccl 8:13

So please skip all the drugs, you'll avoid the pain because
People won't fight with guns; you'll save yourself lots of trouble

The devil tries to amplify your sins to terrify, terrify, terrify
Instead cherish God, glorify, and qualify, qualify, qualify

Let Me Love You

The devil tries to amplify your sins to terrify, terrify, terrify
Instead cherish God, glorify, and qualify, qualify, qualify

Then your health will multiply, you'll find Him
He'll always be near Mount Zion   Rev 14:1
You'll find His supply and your life will simplify   Phil 4:19
You'll get to say goodbye to Mount Sinai   Exod 20

But God

(Adapted from the melody of "Numb" by Linkin Park)

God has made us alive within Christ Eph 2
The battle's not just yours, He can deliver
You're who you are due to His sacrifice
But God choose what's foolish to put shame to the wise
                                                    1 Cor 1:27–31

Witness the light of God
   Be a witness to the light of God 1 John 1:5
But the Word of our LORD God can never become chained down
Witness the light of God, Be a witness to the light of God

God is slow to anger, He remains my strength Ps 145:8
But God is love, He redeems us from death Gal 3:13
Because of His will, Jesus Christ was raised Rom 8:34
Mercy He's rich in, By grace you've been saved Eph 2:8–9

Know that God observes every hardship Ps 139:4
He stands right beside you; He feels all that you do
He'll never leave your side regardless Deut 31:8
His gift is peace, He's good and so loves you John 14:27

Witness the light of God, Be a witness to the light of God
But the Word of our LORD God can never become chained down
Witness the light of God, Be a witness to the light of God
And every second not aligned will be wasteful by design
                                                    Eph 5:11

God is slow to anger, He remains my strength
But God is love, He redeems us from death
Because of His will, Jesus Christ was raised
Mercy He's rich in, By grace you've been saved

Let Me Love You

Though painful
God allowed His Son to be tortured   Isa 53:10
He's faithful
So, you can claim His free gift of eternal life your reward
                                                                    John 3:16

God is slow to anger, He remains my strength
But God is love, He redeems us from death
Because of His will, Jesus Christ was raised
Mercy He's rich in, By grace you've been saved

God is slow to anger, He remains my strength
God has made us alive within Christ

God's Realm

(Adapted from the melody of "Meet Me At Our Spot" by THE ANXIETY)

If you feel stuck	
And you're down on your luck	
Everything seems to obstruct	
Want to enter slumber?	
Might be outnumbered	
Loaded down, encumbered	
Real life makes you humble	
God lives within our hearts	1 John 4:12
He'll be your guide	
There's a special place inside to reside	
This comes to everyone who's baptized	Mark 16:16
He just wants to provide His supply, His supply	
He hears us when we cry	Prov 15:29
Once a man, He can empathize	John 1:14
No need to apologize	
This is the ultimate prize	
And when you're knee-deep	
When you suffer critique	
Get down on your knees and plea	Eph 3:14
Seek the Holiest trustee	
Growing older	
Before your heart is colder	Matt 24:12
He'll grant you a fresh start	2 Cor 5:17–21
God lives within our hearts	

And if in spite
You try to fill that void inside
With something other than His light
Quite frankly, it'll be denied

He knows when we cry
Once a man, He can empathize
No need to apologize
This is the ultimate prize

God lives within our hearts
He really wants to befriend you
God lives within our hearts
Allow Him in or despair

God lives within our hearts
He really wants to befriend you
God lives within our hearts
Allow Him in or despair

He'll be your guide
There's a special place inside to reside
This comes to everyone who's baptized
He just wants to provide His supply, His supply

He knows when we cry
Once a man, He can empathize
No need to apologize
This is the ultimate prize

Today Is the Day of Salvation

(Adapted from the melody of "Diamonds" by Sam Smith)

You've been called	1 Cor 7:17
Don't you ignore Him or withdraw	
He'll keep trying if you stall	Rev 3:20
There are so many riches in store	Ps 37: 4

If you knew
All the things that He endured
And all the promises assured   1 Pet 1:3–4
You would think twice next time you ignore

Nothing today in life is guaranteed	Matt 6:34
Maybe tomorrow will be your final day	
You need to begin to prepare	
In Jesus declare or suffer despair	John 14:6

You possess little control
Your story is already foretold
You need to begin to prepare
In Jesus declare or suffer despair

God wants a relationship with you	1 John 3:1–3
But you have to consent to partake	Rom 10:9–11
There are no grandkids in heaven	
Just sons and daughters	2 Cor 6:17–18
God wants a relationship with you	
Your namesake's not enough for thee	
All you have to do is just believe	Rom 10:9
You must seek the truth	John 14:6
God wants a relationship with you	

Let Me Love You

See the cross
Paid your ransom and He bought　　　　Mark 10:45
Your freedom so you could walk
His righteous path so legally　　　　2 Cor 5:21
He wants to be, He wants to be
Everything to you—namely preeminence　　　　Col 1:15–19

Nothing today in life is guaranteed
Maybe tomorrow will be your final day
You need to begin to prepare
In Jesus declare or suffer despair
You possess little control
Your story is already foretold
You need to begin to prepare
In Jesus declare or suffer despair

God wants a relationship with you
But you have to consent to partake
There are no grandkids in heaven
Just sons and daughters
God wants a relationship with you
Your namesake's not enough for thee
All you have to do is just believe
You must seek the truth
God wants a relationship with you

Don't misconstrue
God wants a relationship with you
Follow through

But you have to consent to partake
There are no grandkids in heaven
Just sons and daughters
God wants a relationship with you
Your namesake's not enough for thee
All you have to do is just believe
You must seek the truth
God wants a relationship with you

Follow through
God wants a relationship with you
Follow through
God wants a relationship with you

One day, you will stand alone   Rom 14:10–12
In front of His judgment throne
Will you choose by works or by faith?

If you choose by works,
The comparison will not be to other people
But rather to God's perfect standard
For whoever keeps the whole law
But fails in one point has become guilty of them all   Jas 2:10

Let Me Love You

Beside

*(Adapted from the melody of "Always on Time"
by Ja Rule, feat. Ashanti)*

I'll be there when you fall, right there just beside   Matt 28:20
Anytime that you call; trust in Me, confide   Prov 3:5
I'll be there when you fall, right there just beside
Anytime that you call, always

Always, I'll be there when you fall, right there just beside
Anytime that you call; trust in Me, confide
I'll be there when you fall, right there just beside
Anytime that you call; trust in Me, confide

When times get tough, and you start to shudder
When there's seems no hope, that's when you discover
There's a solution to your emotional pain
I know you can't help but to take My name in vain   Mark 7:6–9

Nothing seems to negate, but I hear all your complaints
You might think though as God, how can I relate?
But really, I adore
You and your vulnerable heart for sure, won't you agree?

Sometimes you think I'm delayed   2 Pet 3:8–9
But I hear everything each day when you pray   1 Chr 28:9
Ask for anything, please don't be afraid
If it's within My will and purpose, I'll provide   I John 5:14–15
Your trials are mine and I'll make it worthwhile
Give Me a chance to show that you are reconciled   Rom 5:10–11

But, in your despair, I will certainly repair your welfare—I declare

Let Me Love You

Always, I'll be there when you fall, right there just beside
Anytime that you call; trust in Me, confide
I'll be there when you fall, right there just beside
Anytime that you call; trust in Me, confide

When your anger raises your blood pressure
Things seem way out of control, and you resign to whatsoever
Don't throw up your arms and simply surrender
I will direct things around you, and they'll pull
    together   Prov 21:1

You'll see with time, I'll guarantee
You won't be alone; I'll be all that you need
You have to take a chance and learn to trust me   Eph 3:17
I'm closest when you're the most desperately   Jas 1:2–4
I'm your best friend, and not your enemy
You're My son and I'll treat you exceptionally

I will guard, I'll give you the power to conquer
Your wins will be ours; I'll make sure that you'll be honored
Be aware, nothing will ever compare
I will answer your prayers, you'll be in My care   John 5:14–15

But, in your despair, I will certainly repair your welfare—I declare

Always, I'll be there when you fall, right there just beside
Anytime that you call; trust in Me, confide
I'll be there when you fall, right there just beside
Anytime that you call; trust in Me, confide

So, when you're feeling overwhelmed and feeling strife
When today's circumstances undermine
Maybe, ask for My help this time, because I'm divine

Let Me Love You

We're in-line, this time will be a refresher
I'm on your side; and it'll please Me, it'll be My pleasure
I love you, and if you truly love Me, then you'll
    obey Me; precisely　　　　　　　　　　　John 14:15–17

You'll ask in My name if you know what will please Me
I give You My cup, grace, and mercy　　　　　　　　Eph 1:7
I offer you eternal forgiveness
This decree, you can now be My witness　　　　　　Isa 43:10

From now on, don't just simply give-up
I'm the answer you seek; you no longer need to be suspicious
A new frontier, there' nothing to fear
I'll appear in the mirror

Always, I'll be there when you fall, right there just beside
Anytime that you call; trust in Me, confide
I'll be there when you fall, right there just beside
Anytime that you call; trust in Me, confide

I'll be there when you fall, right there just beside
Anytime that you call; trust in Me, confide
I'll be there when you fall, right there just beside
Anytime that you call; trust in Me, confide

Outside of Time

(Adapted from the melody of "Bring Me To Life" by Evanescence)

Have you ever wondered or even thought, have you explored
God as the creator of this world
    and where we might've come from?   Gen 1:1–2
Having this control, completely in charge of the console
Once it's set into motion, there's no need to patrol

Outside of time, He's outside of time   Isa 57:15
Outside of time, He's outside of time strangely
We're created clearly off the mark   2 Tim 3:7
Outside of time; this for everyone, I can't deduct
Ever since time began, surely
These things set into motion cannot be undone

It's like watching from high above, a scene of a city
Complete with a miniaturized scale; a train and its tracks

Outside of time, He's outside of time
Outside of time, He's outside of time strangely
We're created clearly off the mark
Outside of time; this for everyone, I can't deduct
Ever since time began, surely
These things set into motion cannot be undone
A train and its tracks
How can you deny all that He has designed?
A train and its tracks

He knows the beginning from the end as such   Rev 22:13
Set from high above, guarding   Deut 10:14
His plan for you and infinity that lies ahead   Jer 29:11

Let Me Love You

Not bound by time, God is not bound like you and me
Light out of dark, time was also created purposefully   Gen 1:3–25
One day for Him is a thousand years for us   2 Pet 3:8
His timeline's not ours, we have to trust
Today's earth will pass away, He's in control   Matt 5:18
A new heaven and earth, God has a plan to restore;
   a train and its tracks   Rev 21

Outside of time, He's outside of time
Outside of time, He's outside of time strangely
We're created clearly off the mark
Outside of time; this for everyone, I can't deduct
Ever since time began, surely
These things set into motion cannot be undone
A train and its tracks
How can you deny all that He has designed?
A train and its tracks

It's His Design

(Adapted from the melody of "About Damn Time" by Lizzo)

We're all in His flock, and some are quirky	John 10:9–16
It might come as a shock, but life's not a party	

You have to be open and willing	2 Cor 3:16
Your heart has to seek fulfillment	
You have to believe to get this message	Eph 2:8–9
Does this make sense? Do you want to know how?	

Happiness is such an underrated measure
It's way too easy to feel depressed
Life rarely happens like what you see in the movies
Are you feeling the pressure?

It's confusing, but to His delight	
It's so revealing, He loves you despite	Eph 1:5
He made the way by His foresight	John 14:6
It's His design	

It's amusing, deliberate
It's exceeding, His grace on display
He made the way by His foresight
It's His design

Many will stray from Him causing a detrimental	Matt 7:13–14
effect, as if they're in a slump	
Feeling lucky, relying exclusively on chance	
which only leads to anxiousness	

He's the creator, it's His touch	Gen 1:1
Believers are secured in His clutch	Isa 62:3
He looks for you until you're found	Matt 18:12–14
He'll carry you if you allow	Luke 15:3–7

Let Me Love You

Happiness is such an underrated measure
It's way too easy to feel depressed
Life rarely happens like what you see in the movies
Are you feeling the pressure?

It's confusing, but to His delight
It's so revealing, He loves you despite
He made the way by His foresight
It's His design

It's amusing, deliberate
It's exceeding, His grace on display
He made the way by His foresight
It's His design
Enriched

Do you know what's on His mind?
He's searching to reunite, He's searching to reunite
He's searching to reunite, He's searching to reunite
He's searching to reunite, He's searching to reunite
He's made the way by His foresight
It's His design

He's searching to reunite, He's searching to reunite
He's searching to reunite, He's searching to reunite
He's searching to reunite, He's searching to reunite
He made the way by His foresight
It's His design

Enriched
It's His design

Captured in the Stars

(Adapted from the melody of "Last Hurrah" by Bebe Rexha)

Since the beginning in the sky showing
The darkness twinkling, brilliant and glowing
His story is hidden, the constellations tell us;
   it's displaying   Ps 19:1–4

You might consider the sky's so much bigger
Sparkles like glitter next to the Big Dipper
It's not just conjecture from heaven's projector
Yes, recount our LORD's adventure

You might take a moment to explore; it's there if you know what you're looking for

Captured in the stars, set apart
Before the written form, His account
In the stars, God ordained   Gen 15:5
Fortunate for the Bible that now explains   Heb 4:12
In the stars, in the stars

The zodiac's forsaken   Deut 18:10
With Virgo it begins
Passed to others through oral
And with Leo, it ends
This diorama describes His Son's drama
This is God's version of "Once upon a . . ."

You might take a moment to explore; it's there if you know what you're looking for

Let Me Love You

Captured in the stars, set apart
Before the written form, His account
In the stars, God ordained
Fortunate for the Bible that now explains
In the stars, in the stars

You might think that it's strange how the stars could contain Jesus' purpose proclaimed
It's profound!

Captured in the stars, set apart
Before the written form, His account
In the stars, God ordained
Fortunate for the Bible that now explains
In the stars, in the stars

God Stays the Same

(Adapted from the melody of "Grand, Ain't Life Grand?" by Kane Brown)

If you watch the news tonight, it couldn't be clearer
No more enforcing, crime's out of control
I'm trying hard to understand it,
    Christians are on high alert   1 Pet 5:8–9
There'll eventually be a price; things will only worsen
All the social constructs in America are being perverted
                                                          Isa 5: 20–21

People are always looking for something
Anything to satisfy their pleasure
Too many are needlessly suffering
Nothing else is left to be treasured
God stays the same   Heb 13:8

So many people are going to be damned   Ps 88
I've already witnessed too many firsthand
There's way too much sin on-demand
God stays the same

No one cares about finding the Promised Land
No one lends a stranger a helping hand
How much more do you think we can withstand?
Soon, things will change

Norms will rearrange, our culture's reversed what's right and wrong
U.S. cities are run-down
Evil's increasing and Your blessed name's disavowed
There's not much left, exactly how much more are You going to
    allow?
On Your command, the angels will blow
    their trumpets—resound   Rev 8

People are always looking for something
Anything to satisfy their pleasure
Too many are needlessly suffering
Nothing else is left to be treasured
God stays the same

So many people are going to be damned
I've already witnessed too many firsthand
There's way too much sin on-demand
God stays the same

No one cares about finding the Promised Land
No one lends a stranger a helping hand
How much more do you think we can withstand?
Soon, things will change
Indeed, they'll fall; they'll fall down dead
Indeed, they'll fall; they'll fall down dead
Indeed, they'll fall; they'll fall down dead
God stays the same

People are always looking for something
Anything to satisfy their pleasure
Too many are needlessly suffering
Nothing else is left to be treasured
God stays the same

So many people are going to be damned
I've already witnessed too many firsthand
There's way too much sin on-demand
God stays the same

No one cares about finding the Promised Land
No one lends a stranger a helping hand
How much more do you think we can withstand?
Soon, things will change

Indeed, they'll fall; they'll fall down dead
Indeed, they'll fall; they'll fall down dead
Indeed, they'll fall; they'll fall down dead
God stays the same

Indeed, they'll fall; they'll fall down dead
Indeed, they'll fall; they'll fall down dead
Indeed, they'll fall; they'll fall down dead
God stays the same

This Is How God Works

(Adapted from the melody of "You Broke Me First" by Tate McRae)

I'd like to share a short story with you about myself
When I was a teenager, my Mom fought cancer and lost her health
After she died, could I survive? But God turned it round
My life soon changed course and fortunately His plan I found

I lost hope, a dark abyss
I wasn't aware of the spiritual battle that exists;
    but I did, I resisted   Eph 6:12
And learned that everything happens for a reason
                                                      Jer 29:11–13

Then suddenly the devil sends his attack
It strikes its target, but God then counteracts   1 Pet 5:8–9
He takes what was designed solely for bad
And redirects it to make a positive impact   Rom 8:28
This is how God works; this is how God works

In his style sent some trials, the devil tried to subvert
Thought he was punishing Jesus with the cross to assert   Gal 3:13
But God had something else in mind
    instead to save the world   John 3:16–17
"You are not your own," Jesus conveyed   1 Cor 3:23

Forgive them, please do this   Luke 23:34
I asked that You take this cup from Me
But it was not Your wish   Matt 26:39
And Your will, I insist   Matt 26:42
Yes, God plans everything in due season   1 Pet 5:6

Then suddenly the devil sends his attack
It strikes its target, but God then counteracts
He takes what was designed solely for bad
And redirects it to make a positive impact
This is how God works; this is how God works

The same thing to Saul happened
Changed his ways, re-examined   Acts 26:20
From blindness to renewed sight   Acts 9:9
Then preaching grace became his passion   Eph 2:8–9

Then suddenly the devil sends his attack
It strikes its target, but God then counteracts
He takes what was designed solely for bad
And redirects it to make a positive impact
This is how God works; this is how God works

Saving Souls

(Adapted from the melody of "Midnight Sky" by Miley Cyrus)

You can deny all you want that God sits on His throne
Just because you feel that you are in full control
Careful, your thoughts and actions might provoke
It's on you, your decisions; they're your's   Jas 1:5

If we choose to live on our own, we're forsaken   Phil 2:3–4
Our free will He will allow   Job 34:4

God loves everyone, He won't be ignored or outdone, oh no
He wants to reside deep within you
God sent His Son who was cursed on the tree where He hung,
    it's so   John 3:16
He wants to respectfully guide you

There's great sin in being proud, please consider yourself warned
    —maybe
No, don't misconstrue
God loves everyone, He won't be ignored or outdone, oh no
He wants to respectfully guide you, to guide you

Somewhere deep inside is reserved a special place   1 Cor 6:19–20
If you constantly ignore Him, soon it'll be erased
Nothing else will satisfy, then evil will replace
God's in the business of saving souls   Eph 2:8

If we choose to live on our own, we're forsaken
Our free will He will allow

God loves everyone, He won't be ignored or outdone, oh no
He wants to reside deep within you
God sent His Son who was cursed on the tree where He hung, it's so
He wants to respectfully guide you

Let Me Love You

There's great sin in being proud, please consider yourself warned
   —maybe
No, don't misconstrue
God loves everyone, He won't be ignored or outdone, oh no
He wants to respectfully guide you, guide you

If He relaxes His hands, you will fall through, fall through

God loves everyone, He won't be ignored or outdone, oh no
He wants to reside deep within you
God sent His Son who was cursed on the tree where He hung, it's so
He wants to respectfully guide you

He provides the escape; wouldn't you prefer instead to be embraced—maybe?
No, don't misconstrue
God loves everyone, He won't be ignored or outdone, oh no
He wants to respectfully guide you

No, don't misconstrue
No, don't misconstrue
Respectfully guide you

Let Me Love You

I Loved You First

(Adapted from the melody of "My Universe" by Coldplay & BTS)

Know that I, I loved you first	1 John 4:19
And that you are no longer under the curse	Gal 3:13
And know that the curse has been reversed by Christ	
	Rom 5:12–19

Just let go of the things that others do to you	Matt 6:14
Don't hold it against them, don't you despise	
For I am the one whom they'll have to answer	2 Cor 5:10
Because this might destroy you and cause your demise	

Jesus Christ so died	2 Cor 5:21
Glory to Him, you should be praising	
And now He resides beside	1 Pet 3:22
Intercessions He is making	1 John 2:1–2

Know that I, I loved you first
And that you are no longer under the curse
And know that the curse has been reversed by Jesus Christ

Don't be offended by constant oppressors	1 Cor 13:5
Trust that I am good, you are my bride	Eph 5:22–33
Instead, offer grace and be a possessor	
Feel it from within, let Me be your guide	

Know that I, I loved you first
And that you are no longer under the curse
And know that the curse has been reversed by Jesus Christ

You'll be reimbursed	Mark 4:20
You'll be reimbursed	
You'll be reimbursed	
This, you have My Word	

Let Me Love You

Always be slow to anger	Prov 14:29
Remember to love one another	John 13:34
And If you don't forgive others	Eph 4:32
Then I cannot forgive you either	

Deal with things in private	
If received, then you've gained a brother	Matt 18:15–20
If not, then approach with others	
If to no avail, then leave it to themselves to suffer	2 Cor 6:17

It's peace that you'll find	John 14:27
Regardless of what you're facing	
Be thankful and be kind	1 Thess 5:16–18
The end result will be amazing	

Know that I, I loved you first
And that you are no longer under the curse
And know that the curse has been reversed by Jesus Christ

You'll be reimbursed
You'll be reimbursed
You'll be reimbursed
This, you have My Word

God So Loves You

(Adapted from the melody of "The Lost Room" by Pet Shop Boys)

It all seems way too cruel	
Why God would sacrifice His Son for us to be redeemed	Rom 5:8; Rom 3:22–24
This world, there's no regard	2 Cor 5:16
Oblivious to His grace and mercy; no faith, no belief	Heb 11:6
Betrayed—they feel in contrary	
God so loves you; don't be dismayed	John 3:16
Jesus freely obeyed His Father fully knowing what was arranged	John 13:3
God so loves you; don't be afraid	Isa 41:10
The power of God to salvation; for the gospel I'm not ashamed	Rom 1:16
Discover what is the truth	John 14:6
Admit that He's the King of kings and worthy of glory and praise	Rev 19:16
Uncover what the Bible says	
In the beginning was the Word; His flesh died and then was raised	John 1:1
Your soul—the beneficiary	
God so loves you; it's guaranteed	
All things will be given to you if His kingdom and Righteousness you seek	Matt 6:33
God so loves you, for eternity	1 Chr 16:34
There'll be darkness in His absence and your future will be bleak	1 John 1:5–10

Let Me Love You

Turn and then repent	Acts 3:19–21
Be baptized to receive the Holy Spirit, this is what I pray	Acts 2:38
Christ, do you accept?	
Jesus bore your condemnation because He died in your place	2 Cor 5:21
Today—you have been saved	Eph 2:8–10

God so loves you; don't be dismayed
Jesus freely obeyed His Father fully knowing what was arranged
God so loves you; don't be afraid
The power of God to salvation; for the gospel I'm not ashamed

God so loves you; it's guaranteed
All things will be given to you if His kingdom and
    Righteousness you seek
In the Spirit, the flesh—farewell   Gal 5:16
You'll find refuge under His wings where forever you will dwell
                                                                 Ps 91:4

You're bought, because of the cross   1 Cor 6:20
You're bought, because of the cross

THE BIBLE

The Mysteries of the Bible

(Adapted from the melody of "Nobody Gets Me" by Sza)

Most people just don't care; don't disrupt, just leave them
They live their lives oblivious, unaware that they're condemned
Focused only on the pointless; not for me, because I've been searching
for God's mysteries cause I'm yearning for an understanding and discernment

Indeed, God's great
There's no acceptable excuse—only His truth   John 17:17
The mysteries of the Bible are revealed
In the types and examples that He shares
For yourself, only you can choose   Deut 30:15

If you seek His wisdom, all else flows   Matt 6:33
In Christ's likeness to reproduce   2 Cor 3:18
Do you want to live carefree? Look to His fruit   Prov 7:2
Do you want to live carefree? Look to His fruit
Do you want to live carefree? Look to His fruit
Do you want to live carefree?

His path is the narrow way   Matt 7:13–14
The rapture and just faith can save   Eph 2:8–9
Jews and Gentiles in one body   Gal 3:28
The Church and the Holy Spirit that completes   Eph 5:22–33

All my sins and errors I'll confess   1 John 1:9
for Your approval; soon heaven's kingdom
With Your help and blessings, I can; it's true
There's so much to contemplate

There's no acceptable excuse—only His truth
The mysteries of the Bible are revealed in the types and examples
that He shares
For yourself, only you can choose

If you seek His wisdom, all else flows
In Christ's likeness to reproduce

Do you want to live carefree? Look to His fruit
Do you want to live carefree? Look to His fruit
Do you want to live carefree? Look to His fruit
Do you want to live carefree?

You Have to Recognize

(Adapted from the melody of "Apologize" by Timbaland & OneRepublic)

When things occur in your life
When things happen and confound
You have to be able to decipher
The root cause and then rebound

The devil likes to move you in circles
Like on a merry-go-round; he sets his bait   Jer 5:26
Whereas God might allow this   Job 1:12
But He will always surround those who obey Him   1 John 5:1–5

But it's crucial that you recognize, you have to
But it's crucial that you recognize, you have to

The devil's an imitator
All he can do to you is pursue
You need to realize this
Stop running and rebuke to undue   Jas 4:7

If you really know your Bible
Then you'll have a clue—everyday   Heb 4:12
You'll know deep down inside who's the source   Luke 17:21
And then see though the devil's charade

But it's crucial that you recognize, you have to
But it's crucial that you recognize, you have to

But it's crucial that you recognize, you have to
But it's crucial that you recognize, you have to

But it's crucial that you recognize, you have to
But it's crucial that you recognize, you have to

Let Me Love You

When things occur in your life
When things happen and confound . . .

The Light of the Gospel

(Adapted from the melody of "Cold Heart" by Elton John & Dua Lipa [PNAU remix])

It's by God's design	
Hopefully not lifelong	
With a veil placed to blind you	2 Cor 3:14
His elect only to belong	Matt 22:14
Those chosen are marked, if only you knew	Rev 9:4
They're aware of the truth, yes certainly	
You need a breakthrough	
It's not where you start, but rather how far you climb	
Not according to your failures that ultimately defines	
It's how your race ends that dictates if you go home	2 Tim 4:7
It's so, it's so	
You could believe all the garbage instead	
And surrender your spirit apart from God dead	
Those chosen are marked, if only you knew	
They're aware of the truth, yes certainly	
You need a breakthrough	
Just to focus only on the Old Testament's a crime	
Second Corinthians verse 3:14 states they're blind	2 Cor 3:14
Removed only by Christ's atonement	1 John 2:2
It's so, it's so	
Consider the New Testament to be fed	Rom 5:8
To see the light of the gospel and your veil will be shed	
Those chosen are marked, if only you knew	
They're aware of the truth, yes certainly	
You need a breakthrough	

Let Me Love You

There are many misconceptions 'bout God that blaspheme
Perversions of the truth that if one knows the Bible scream
Directed to the wilderness to wander and roam　　　Exod 16
It's so, it's so
Do not be gullible, don't be misled
(Just to focus only on the Old Testament's a crime)
The elect are covered in His bloodshed
(Second Corinthians verse 3:14 states they're blind)
It's so, it's so

Assured, assured, assured, assured
It's so, it's so

Let Me Love You

The Bible's Your Basic Guide

(Adapted from the melody of "Ghost" by Justin Bieber)

You're worth more than a flock of sparrows	Matt 10:29–31
Do not fear, no need for sorrow	Isa 41:10
He gives us all things because He has borrowed	
You know He paid all our debts, please don't forget	Luke 7:42–43
I just want you to grow	Eph 4:15
So, if you want to start anew	2 Cor 5:17
You have to let Him into you	John 14:23
The Bible's your basic guide, your basic guide	Ps 119:105

Especially if you're feeling helplessly
Being attacked by the enemy
The Bible's your basic guide
The Bible's your basic guide

If you look for the signs, they will foreshadow	
There's no need to hide, there's nothing He doesn't know	1 John 3:20
The closer you get, then it seems more arrows	Rev 12:12
You only get one chance, please don't regret	
I just want you to grow	

So, if you want to start anew
You have to let Him into you
The Bible's your basic guide

Especially if you're feeling helplessly
Being attacked by the enemy
The Bible's your basic guide
The Bible's your basic guide

LET ME LOVE YOU

The Bible's your basic guide

So, if you want to start anew
You have to let Him into you
The Bible's your basic guide

Especially if you're feeling helplessly
Being attacked by the enemy
The Bible's your basic guide
The Bible's your basic guide

Feed on Good Food

(Adapted from the melody of "So Good" by Halsey)

Some argue, some cite that the Bible's overrated
And then others recite that it's outdated
Some even try to rewrite it; the Word of God is so hated
Did you ever wonder why?

"Don't fear," these are the words of Jesus	Luke 12:32
Trust that He is the wisest; this you can count on	

He was pressed, yet He was resurrected	Rom 6:8–11
Full disclosure, it was His blood smeared on the doorposts	Exod 12:7
that the angel of death purposefully passed over	Exod 12:12–13
Avoid yeast for leaven is symbolic of sin and not kosher	Exod 12:17–20

In historic terms, the Bible's the most important book	
Much to be glad, the Bible's full of good food	Matt 4:4

You can fool yourself and deny and then slowly decay	
But instead, if you apply, then there's great success to claim	
The secret's His ways whereby all of His grace transferring	2 Cor 12:9–10
Tapped into an endless supply	

"Come near"; you are righteous and so blessed	2 Cor 5:21
Wearing salvation's garments, living waters drawn	Isa 61:10; John 7:38
Nothing ever comes close, none since	
Please, don't remain ignorant; all of this, I'll bestow	

He was pressed, yet He was resurrected
Full disclosure, it was His blood on the doorposts

Let Me Love You

In historic terms, the Bible's the most important book
Much to be glad, the Bible's full of good food

For those of you who are feeling downtrodden and wearied
When there seems no escape and when things get kind of scary
There is an answer and Jesus will provide the way   John 14:6
All you have to do is proclaim, He'll protect you
   from Judgment Day   Luke 6:37–38

He was pressed, yet He was resurrected
Full disclosure, it was His blood on the doorposts
In historic terms, the Bible's the most important book
Much to be glad, the Bible's full of good food

SURRENDERING

A New Opportunity

(Adapted from the melody of "Under the Influence" by Chris Brown)

This is worth discussing
I find myself trapped in a bed today after a freak accident
A consequence of my own folly
What's done is done; I hope I'm gonna be alright, alright, alright

How did this happen? God, what's your plan?
Many unknowns I now face and racing thoughts
Will this repair?
What burdens might bear?
I pray for Your love and grace

I took for granted my immunity	Isa 54:17
I thought I was protected truthfully	2 Thess 3:3
Recently I lived my life quite foolishly	
A new beginning, a new opportunity	2 Cor 5:17

Will You forgive me? When will You acquit?	
Lesson learned, we're all hypocrites	Rom 3:23–24
Many things in this life contradict	
Anything in place of You is counterfeit	Exod 20:3–6

I know it's crazy; it's all in the open, not incognito
I can only blame myself; it's all in the open, not incognito

How did this happen? God, what's your plan?
Many unknowns I now face and racing thoughts
Will this repair?
What burdens might bear?
I pray for Your love and grace

LET ME LOVE YOU

I took for granted my immunity
I thought I was protected truthfully
Recently I lived my life quite foolishly
A new beginning, a new opportunity

How did this happen? God, what's your plan?
Many unknowns I now face and racing thoughts
Will this repair?
What burdens might bear?
I pray for Your love and grace

"I Can't"

(Adapted from the melody of "Stand Back" by Stevie Nicks)

By myself, what's this imply
Going it alone is not by His design   Isa 41:10
Although I try, let me explain
I think I'm so smart, but it's insane

You think you know what's ideal
You win some, you lose some; but you're still so confined
This realization finally comes eventually
Don't misunderstand, God's in control   Eph 1:11

"I can't, I can't"
If you want to go through, then you have to surrender too
          Ps 37:7
And despite this, to His delight
Authentic and genuine, authentic and genuine   Rom 12:9
Accept help and resign—realign   Matt 16:24

On my own, I hit a dead-end; I need Your help, on God I depend
With this, there's no shame; I just proclaim

When things fall apart, and I start to feel destitute
I look to Him for a solution; His blessings
    will pursue   Num 6:24–26
When there's another curve ball, ask God from above
    and then you're walking tall

"I can't, I can't"
If you want to go through, then you have to surrrender too
And despite this, to His delight
Authentic and genuine, authentic and genuine
Accept help and resign—realign

Let Me Love You

When things fall apart, and I start to feel destitute
I look to Him for a solution; His blessings will pursue
When there's another curve ball, ask God from above and then you're walking tall

"I can't, I can't"
If you want to go through, then you have to surrrender too
And despite this, to His delight
Authentic and genuine, authentic and genuine
Accept help and resign—realign

What if you saw things differently? What if you saw things differently?
"I can't." What if you saw things differently? "I can't"

Let Me Love You

Broken

(Adapted from the melody of "Golden" by Harry Styles)

Broken, broken, broken
Can't do this on my own
Frozen, stolen, choking
I'm feeling alone
I know I'm nothing without You by myself   John 15:4–5
I'm hopeless, broken   Ps 34:18
I'm just not quite like anyone else
Born to fail despite
I'm so broken

I'm so broken
I'm lost
No map to guide, roaming
Before You've spoken

I know that I'm not alone, I know that I'm not alone   Ps 23
It's like you're speaking to me through headphones
I know that I'm not alone
But I'd prefer to wear a blindfold (I'll wear a blindfold)
A steep price I've paid for (a steep price I've been paid for)
                                                   1 Tim 2:6
And I'm grateful to have found Your throne   Rev 5:13
Loving you achieves my pardon   1 John 1:9

Broken, I'm so broken
I know that I'm not alone
I'm so broken

I'm so broken
I know that I'm spared   Rom 3:21–26
And I'm saved just as You've declared   Acts 2:37–41
Because I'm so broken

Let Me Love You

I know that I'm spared
Because I'm so broken
I'm so broken
I know that I'm not alone
I'm so broken, I'm so broken, I'm so broken
I'm know that I'm spared

And I'm saved just as You've declared
Because I'm so broken

Broken, but Renewed

(Adapted from the melody of "Eyes Without A Face" by Billy Idol)

I find myself without hope
Kneeling in church
I sit up front

People walk around
Don't mind me deep in thought
Trying to find my way

It's easy to surrender
But hard to let go
Just when you've hit your low

You are not alone; Father, please help me   Ps 23
You are not alone; Father, please help me
You are not alone; Father, please help me
I need You to heal me; Father, please help me

I spend every week here
I'm sobbing all the time
After the communion

This is my special time
I feel so close to You
I'm still so vulnerable

You are not alone; Father, please help me
You are not alone; Father, please help me
You are not alone; Father, please help me
I need You to heal me; Father, please help me

Let Me Love You

When I hear the guitar, I start to slip
Into deep meditation—a faraway trip
You come into focus, face to face   2 Cor 4:6
I receive Your grace   2 Cor 12:9

I sense that I'm being held so tight
Turning deep sorrow into delight
Chewing Your host, I find insight   Matt 26:26–30

I look forward every week to share our time
Waiting patiently for You to send me a sign
I'm thinking of You and Your love, always—so

I say my prayers
I say my prayers
I say my prayers

When I close my eyes
I can see You clearly
I know that You're near me   Ps 145:18

Now all I want to do
Is change my future path
And just follow You   Luke 18:22
But it's going to be a long road
But I feel like I'm prepared

You are not alone; Father, please help me
You are not alone; Father, please help me
You are not alone; Father, please help me
I need You to heal me; Father, please help me

All the hurt stings less   1 Cor 15:55–57
I think I passed this test   John 16:33
I know that I am blessed   Num 6:24–26

My Life Is Your Life

I can't remember my younger self
I simply refuse
As I've changed so much when I dealt
With death's abuse just to improve — Ps 34:18

Your ways I hold myself — Jer 26:12–13
Do You really approve?
Serving upheld

Oh, it's Your life
Won't You descend?
My life is Your life — Ps 25:1–12
Help me ascend (help me ascend) — Ps 24:3–6

Grateful that You brought me to the end of myself — 2 Cor 3:18
I got the clue
You allowed the worst for the best compelled
Another chance to renew — 2 Cor 4:16

Oh, please use myself
Just as Your own vessel — Isa 42:6
Work through myself

Oh, it's Your life
Won't You descend?
My life is Your life
Help me ascend (help me ascend)

And I pray to excel
All praise goes to You — Ps 105:1–2
And glory for Yourself

Let Me Love You

Oh, it's Your life
Won't You descend?
My life is Your life
Help me ascend (help me ascend)

Oh, it's Your life
I have no regrets
Caught up in the clouds
My spirit transcends, my spirit transcends   Ps 148:13

Stretch Marks

(Adapted from the melody of "Closer" by Nine Inch Nails)

A trial appears out of the blue	Jas 1:2–4
You have to change your point of view	
An explanation is overdue	
But remember who you're talking to	Isa 46:9
Nothing really comes as a surprise	Ps 147:5
Nothing from you will be withheld	2 Pet 1
Nothing will be revealed until it's time	
"Nothing" will be used to propel	
These experiences are so valuable	
If you just let Jesus be your guide	Ps 32:8; Is 58:11
While in the midst, it may feel radical	
But you'll be amazed at what it unlocks	
Proudly display your stretch marks	
Trials can be used to strengthen	Jas 1:2–8
Although at that time they sting	
Your perception and your attitude really matter	Eph 4:23–24
It's the sum of all these things	
Loving, there'll soon be a completion	
Loving, evil spirits expelled	Mark 16:17
Loving, your body's a temple	1 Corinthians 6:19–20
Loving means God wants to indwell	1 Corinthians 3:16

These experiences are so valuable
If you just let Jesus be your guide
While in the midst, it may feel radical
But you'll be amazed at what it unlocks
Proudly display your stretch marks

Let Me Love You

Our human existence, despite disease, is a test in and of itself	Deut 8:2
He hears your pleas, you are a spirit	Prov 15:29
You will ultimately survive	John 11:25–26
Supplied a new body	Phil 3:21
Your soul will thrive	3 John 1:2

Let Me Love You

Faith Possessor

(Adapted from the melody of "All Of Me" by John Legend)

How many times have I acted so proud?
Following the Pharisees' ways, I espoused — Matt 6:5
Focused on flesh living, I was unwilling; I need to rebound

Early in life, I used to be blind — John 9:25
I'm grateful that my life has realigned
I was too busy, or at least in theory; and this by Your design
— Rom 8:28

I used to be an imposter, but now I've resigned
I've surrendered and now You're the headline — Jas 4:7

Cause morally, I acknowledge You
I'm not just a faith professor — 2 Sam 2:26
But instead, a faith possessor — Eph 1:8

You're my priority — Col 1:18
How can I live up to You?
You're the solution to all my sinning — Rom 10:9–10
You paid the price; You're so forgiving — John 3:16
You grant all of this lawfully — John 3:17
Each day You allow me to renew, oh — Ezek 36:26

So many times, on my knees I begged You — Eph 3:14–21
To fix everything and expected You to
Your grace continually abounds, a downfall
   of heavy rain I conclude — Rom 5:20

You bore all sickness; Your body bruised — Isa 53:5
The greatest transaction, yet You made no excuse — Luke 22:42
Since the beginning, You were willing; diseases
   have been loosed — Luke 13:12

Let Me Love You

I used to be an imposter
But now I've resigned
I've surrendered and now You're the headline

Cause morally, I acknowledge You
I'm not just a faith professor
But instead, a faith possessor

You're my priority
How can I live up to You?
You're the solution to all my sinning
You paid the price; You're so forgiving
You grant all of this lawfully
Each day You allow me to renew, oh

It's not that "I love You"
But that You truly loved me; You're the real source
    of truth   1 John 4:19–20
And I'm thankfully one of Your body parts   1 Cor 12:27

Cause morally, I acknowledge You
I'm not just a faith professor
But instead, a faith possessor

You're my priority
How can I live up to you?
You're the solution to all my sinning
You paid the price; You're so forgiving
You grant all of this lawfully
Each day You allow me to renew, oh

You grant all of this lawfully
Each day You allow me to renew, oh

LET ME LOVE YOU

The Purpose of Suffering

(Adapted from the melody of "Silent Lucidity" by Queensrÿche)

When life's good, no sighs
Or if you've never felt completely empty inside
No hunger or no dread
Or never experienced a loved one on their deathbed

If it's always sunny and never rains
If you're never in a corner, why seek help or explain . . . these things
Finite world, life occurs by chance
There's nothing weighing on you today
Free and careless
Until something confronts   1 Pet 1:7

Difficulties are going to arise   John 16:33
Life changes course and thus comes as a surprise
Not ready, not prepared
Your comfortable life has suddenly disappeared

When there's nowhere left to turn
Open your eyes wide to discern   Matt 13:9–16
Look deep inside your heart

Exposed and so vulnerable
Masterfully, an answer appears   Matt 7:7
Your life finds a new direction   Isa 30:21

I-I see there's a purpose in review   Rom 5:12
I-I now know You were in pursuit   Luke 19:10
I-I understand why You hid from sight   Rev 3:20
I-I received Your hand outstretched when I
    suffered my defeat   John 6:44

Let Me Love You

When you're brought down to your knees
And your soul cries out desperately with your
    pleas   Eccl 3:1
You're given a choice therein
Your free will expressed; doors open, and winds shift   Acts 2:2

Stability and happiness return
Your problems are no longer just your own   1 Pet 5:7
Rely on His supply   Phil 4:19

The person you were once is now dead   Col 3:3–5
A permanent invitation to heaven   Matt 11:28
Whereby you've arrived; He'll be nearby and . . .   Luke 23:36–43

I-I see there's a purpose in review
I-I now know You were in pursuit
I-I understand why You hid from sight
I-I received Your hand outstretched . . .

Right There Beside

(Adapted from the melody of "Moth to a Flame" by Swedish House Mafia & The Weeknd)

My life's been mundane
My problems have been minor up to this point and have affected me minimally
I'm a Christian just in name
But I lack insight and resiliency
I'm at the end of my rope literally

I should have known that I was overdue
Something serious has finally broken through
The beginning of the end has now begun
I'm not sure what will ensue

Now, I must determine what are my real beliefs
Now more than ever, I need my faith to increase
I wasn't prepared; this came as a surprise to me
Is this one final attempt by the Holy Spirit in disguise?   Rom 8:28
He's right there beside   Phil 4:4–7

Is this by chance? Or is this by His design?
Is it deliberate perhaps?

The writing's on the wall—a preview
I'm afraid it's too late to undue
Some friends and my loved ones are camped nearby
I will need to pass through   Ps 23:1–4

Let Me Love You

This is a real test causing suffering and grief
I'm praying constantly to receive His grace and
   His peace   1 Thess 5:16–17
I'm not alone; I can no longer deny   Isa 41:10
It's time to surrender; in God I truly confide   Matt 11:28
He's right there beside

He has forgiven me clearly; He's right there beside
He is so near; He's right there beside

He continues to amaze me

He's right there beside; He's right there beside
He's right there beside; He's right there beside

THE CHURCH

Let Me Love You

Passive Christians

(Adapted from the melody of "la di die" by Nessa Barrett, feat. Jaden Hossler [DVBBS remix])

Do you fear what they did to Stephen?
The first martyr who was stoned
"Do not hold this sin against them"   Acts 7:54–60
This was the prayer that he moaned

False accusations of public blasphemy
Required for his deathblow
But he still spoke the truth
All of this at the feet of Saul

Do you think you would've fled?
Or stayed to defend?
Are you willing to be pressed?
Exactly what are you willing to stand for?

Are you scared to be spit on?   Matt 26:67
Prefer to watch from afar?
Or do you have the courage to be bold
And reject the status quo?

Are you afraid that you might die?
Only you can decide
With courage, you can inspire
Not sorry; you must opine
You must opine, you must opine

The world's only getting darker
Words are only getting sharper
Soon there'll be a world order
Then chaos followed by mass disorder

Let Me Love You

It takes effort to include
It's easy to make an excuse
You have protection; you've got to be stern
You have protection   Ps 91:4

Have concessions? Use your discretion
Offer the ultimate love expression
If you seek heaven, share your confession   Jas 5:16
If you seek heaven, share your confession

Are you scared to be spit on?
Prefer to watch from afar?
Or do you have the courage to be bold
And reject the status quo?

Are you afraid that you might die?
Only you can decide
With courage, you can inspire
Not sorry; you must opine

Are you afraid that you might die?
Only you can decide
With courage, you can inspire
Not sorry; you must opine

Are you afraid that you might die?
Only you can decide
With courage, you can inspire
Not sorry; you must opine

Before you turn the corner
Consider this before you flee
Nothing in this life is guaranteed   John 12:25
Your consciousness can be free

Let Me Love You

And when you encounter any drama
You have to demonstrate composure
Leave a permanent impression
Your rewards will be bestowed   1 Thess 2:19

Do you think you would've fled?
Or stayed to defend?
Are you willing to be pressed?
Exactly what are you willing to stand for?

Are you scared to be spit on?
Prefer to watch from afar?
Or do you have the courage to be bold
And reject the status quo?

Are you afraid that you might die?
Only you can decide
With courage, you can inspire
Not sorry; you must opine

The Seven Churches

(Adapted from the melody of "Heat Waves" by Glass Animals)

Let me be clear—Listen to what the Spirit says:
Whoever has ears, let them hear   Mark 4:9
Let me be clear—Listen to what the Spirit says:
Whoever has ears, let them hear

Right now, the timing's opportune
Ephesus, some of you are marooned   Rev 2:1–7
Truth and love, they need to sprout
Versus neglected love, checked-out

Smyrna, a spiritual tycoon   Rev 2:8–11
Faced an insidious typhoon
Its persecution will shortly burn-out
Please remain faithful throughout

In the Book of Revelation's recordings
Present-day Christians are given warnings
Prophetic advice in written letters
Luring us away from our faith
Stressing these four things:

The Holy Spirit offered this premise   Rev 1:1–20
It seized the Apostle John on Patmos
Write down what you see
And send these to the seven churches

Pergamos and its pervasive communes   Rev 2:12–17
Compromising moral buffoons
You have to repent aloud
Judgment from the sword of My mouth

Let Me Love You

You mustn't argue,
You must believe   John 20:30–31
My Righteousness you can become
I want to let you know
My judgment, only I can undo   Zeph 3:15
Since My Son has atoned   Gal 1:4
You know I'm coming for you

This message is clear, don't deny
I'm knocking on the door, please reply   Rev 3:20

Thyatira, faith and service you grew   Rev 2:18–29
But stumbled with idolatry, skewed
False teachings and prophets avowed
Not to mention corruption allowed

Sardis appeared alive but doomed   Rev 3:1–6
Repent before the thief comes through
You just faked being devout
Going through the motions without

Don't you wonder what's the meaning of   Rev 3:3–4
when I make you sad and vulnerable?
You need to make the changes I ask;
time to rest and worship on the Sabbath   Deut 5:12

Weakened **Philadelphia** who knew?   Rev 3:7–13
Faithful to God in lieu
Blessings and praises laid out
My perseverance espoused . . .

You'll be protected, attended-to
Spared from tribulations that are due
Your persecutors taken-out
Pillars in heaven no doubt

LET ME LOVE YOU

Lukewarm **Laodicea** will be spewed   Rev 3:14–22
Wealthy, but bankrupt—deja vu
Complacency soon worn-out
Seek the LORD; or it's lights-out

Let me be clear—Listen to what the Spirit says:
Whoever has ears, let them hear
Let me be clear—Listen to what the Spirit says:
Whoever has ears, let them hear

It's Done

(Adapted from the melody of "Alone" by Heart)

The religions of the world are mocked
There is no walk, just a bunch of talk
But one philosophy shines bright
It's the only one that can reunite

Christianity stands by itself—solo
Instead of a do, do, do motto
It's done   John 3:17

It's from the mystery of the triune   Gen 1:26
We're not under the Law, but rather grace and truth   Rom 6:14
It's God's only and begotten Son

Because of Jesus, it's done
Because of Jesus, it's done

Religions require actions on your behalf
Otherwise, you cannot walk upright
No one's perfect, there's no circumstance
Where you can achieve this; it must indict

There's one answer, there's only one
This plan was made before time began
It's done   Gen 1:1

It's from the mystery of the triune
We're not under the Law, but rather grace and truth
It's God's only and begotten Son   John 3:16

Because of Jesus, it's done
Because of Jesus, it's done

LET ME LOVE YOU

Because of Jesus, it's done
Because of Jesus, it's done
It's done, it's done

You Can Come Directly to Me

(Adapted from the melody of "Overpass Graffiti" by Ed Sheeran)

Why are you so afraid?
It's when you only want something
Or need something

That you finally pray
When it's ignored, then it's frustration
And always falling short of

A relationship is all that I ask	Col 3:1–3
So that I can bless you one hundredfold	Matt 19:29
Behold	

I want to make you a bright lamppost	
To shine all through the night uttermost	
To be a blessing for people, then you can approach	Prov 11:25

Heaven's riches will generously rain down on the earth	Isa 44:3–4
To become a son (or daughter) instead of a servant, maybe then perhaps	Gal 4:7
You can't see the Kingdom of God without a rebirth	John 3:3

I'll live inside of you and whisper	Rom 8:9–11
You have to believe before you can receive	Matt 21:22
Beloved, you can come directly to me	Jas 4:8

I have a purpose for you	Jer 29:11
Not just merely an acquaintance	
But rather consecrated	

A change is underway	
To be bold and courageous	Heb 4:16
Forever gracious	

LET ME LOVE YOU

You're my own, you're now called   Gal 1:15–16
I'll promise to no longer withhold
Unfold

I'll answer your prayers before you know   1 John 5:14–15
Reconciliation, eyelashes up close
You are now my elect, may I propose?   2 Tim 1:9

Heaven's riches will generously rain down on the earth
To become a son (or daughter) instead of a servant,
   maybe then perhaps
You can't see the Kingdom of God without a rebirth
I'll live inside of you and whisper
You have to believe before you can receive
Beloved, you can come directly to me
Directly to me

Beloved, you can come directly to me
Directly to me

Heaven's riches will generously rain down on the earth
To become a son (or daughter) instead of a servant, maybe then
   perhaps
You can't see the Kingdom of God without a rebirth

I'll live inside of you and whisper
You have to believe before you can receive
Beloved, you can come directly to me

Yeah, yeah, yeah
Yeah, yeah, yeah
Directly to me

A son instead of a servant, maybe then perhaps

Time to Ripe

(Adapted from the melody of "The Hype" by Twenty One Pilots)

There's something that I'm hoping to clarify
Life as a Christian needn't be immobilized
Just like caring for the vine to grow tasty grapes
Fruits will ripen in their season but time it takes

If you stay attached to the source, it will be supplied
It takes some time to ripe
Keep yourself connected to Him; in Him you'll
    reside   John 15:5–6; Gal 3:26–28
It takes some time to ripe

Just like a shepherd, His sheep desire to be led
Allow Him to provide your needs, you must depend
And during a hot summer day, a tree will thirst
But you'll be planted by a stream with your
    roots dispersed   Jer 17:7–8

Nothing grows overnight, one day at a time
It takes some time to ripe
Grow and develop into Christ's bride; try to
    coincide   Eph 5:22–33
It takes some time to ripe

Now, if Jesus leads you to it
Indeed, He will lead you through (it)   Ps 23
Now, if Jesus leads you to it
Indeed, He will lead you through (it)

But generally, it's a slow process by design
It takes some time to ripe
And then before you realize it, you'll be purified
Transformed and dignified

Let Me Love You

You'll know them by their fruits when they are
    applied   Matt 7:15–20
It takes some time to ripe
Surrender and be Christ occupied; helping others
    qualify   Phil 3:7–9; Matt 28:19–20
It takes some time to ripe

And then the time will come when you'll be beautified
It takes some time to ripe
Share your journey and testify and you'll be
    satisfied   Acts 10:42–43
It takes some time to ripe

The Seal of God

(Adapted from the melody of "My Immortal" by Evanescence)

I can sense Your Spirit near
I'm astonished that You answered some of my
    prayers   Matt 7:7
And I've believed
I've claimed Your gifts and have received   Col 3:23–24
You know my heart's sincere
And You have never postponed

Your ways You have revealed; all I can do is kneel
You surround me with love and a warm embrace   John 3:16

On my head, the seal of God suddenly appears   Tim 2:19
Your protection and identification so revered
You own me and my imperfections disappear
Satan sees this and has . . . to flee

You've guaranteed my eternal safety as a gift of my new birthright
It's invisible; Your authority's behind
I lack nothing, and You lead me beside peaceful streams   Ps 23
I've inherited the kingdom of God; I've become Your appointee

Your ways You have revealed; all I can do is kneel
You surround me with love and a warm embrace

On my head, the seal of God suddenly appears
Your protection and identification so revered
You own me and my imperfections disappear
Satan sees this and has . . . to flee

Placed on me is the Robe of Righteousness; You have
  adorned   Isa 61:10
The hope of heaven is really mine; Your precious Word has so
  been sworn

On my head, the seal of God suddenly appears
Your protection and identification so revered
You own me and my imperfections disappear
Satan sees this and has . . . to flee

About the Author

Eric Zack is a born-again Christian who resorted to poetry as his preferred emotional outlet at the age of twenty years old. At that time, his dear mother died from metastatic cancer at the age of thirty-nine years old. His mother's cancer was not directly talked about in the open with him or his three younger brothers, although she was diagnosed several years before her death. He was raised in a stable middle-class home environment in a small town in the middle of the United States in the Roman Catholic faith and served as an altar boy for several years growing up. He had a difficult time processing what had happened and stepped away from his faith temporarily as he coped and adjusted with this "new normal." Fortunately, he soon returned to his faith with a renewed passion to develop a closer relationship with his Savior Jesus Christ while trying to better understand life, suffering, loss, and healing. His personal mission statement and professional goals have been to "make a difference and help others" because he was not able to do so for his mother.

Since a young age, Eric has generally possessed an introvert personality type and has often kept his thoughts and feelings private for the most part until now. He is also an experienced and expert oncology nurse and nursing college professor in response to his mom's death, which occurred during his third year of college. Today, he is married and has four adult children, none of whom have ever met his mother. Eric's poetry has dealt with most aspects of living life and covers many different, unique topics that most human beings will experience. More recently, he has been driven to write about many aspects of his maturing Christian faith. He noted a significant gap in the literature in regard to Christian poetry that is supported by the Holy Bible and the many truths that the Holy Bible shares. As a result, he wanted to publish his poetry collections to share with whomever is interested in learning more about these topics, whomever enjoys reading and meditating on various Bible verses, and whomever enjoys poetry in general. He felt it a priority at this time in his life to pursue publishing these five volumes to help others in their spiritual journeys given today's serious crises and waning timeline.

His other poetry collections that are not directly related to Christianity may be published at a future date. Eric's poetry style is typically rhythmic and rhyming in nature with repeated chorus lines (almost like a song) to support certain important aspects worth stressing. Up to this point, his poems have been hidden from all and considered amateur (never shared or published before). This has been his "quiet" passion for over thirty years now; and he hopes that some good may come out of him sharing these authentic, cherished poems that are very personal and private in nature. He sincerely believes that the Holy Spirit has coauthored most of these, using him as a vessel to reach others who are in desperate need of answers and/or support.

Thank you for allowing small pieces of me and my life's insight into your reality and life. And may Jesus Christ have all the power, praise, and glory for doing so. And may God continue to bless you and your loved ones as you seek to get closer and closer to Him. In Christ Jesus, Eric.

www.ingramcontent.com/pod-product-compliance
Lightning Source LLC
Chambersburg PA
CBHW060401050426
42449CB00009B/1852